SNOW WHITE

AND THE SEVEN DWARFS

FREELY TRANSLATED
AND ILLUSTRATED BY

WANDA GÁG

This edition published in 1999 by SMITHMARK Publishers,
a division of U.S. Media Holdings, Inc.,
115 West 18th Street, New York, NY 10011.

SMITHMARK Books are available for bulk purchase for sales
promotion and premium use. For details write or call the manager of special sales, SMITHMARK
Publishers, 115 West 18th Street, New York, NY 10011.

ISBN: 0-7651-0860-7

Printed in Hong Kong

10 9 8 7 6 5 4 3 2 1

Library of Congress Catalog Card Number 98-60768

FOR PAT AND JANEY

SNOW WHITE AND THE
SEVEN DWARFS

ONCE upon a time, in the middle of winter, the snow-flakes were falling like feathers from the sky. At a castle window framed in ebony sat a young Queen working at her embroidery, and as she was stitching away and gazing at the snowflakes now and then, she pricked her finger and three little drops of blood fell down upon the snow. And because the red color looked so beautiful there on the snow she thought to herself, "Oh, if I only had a little child as white as snow, as rosy red as blood, and with hair as ebon black as the window frame!"

Soon after this a baby girl was born to her—a little Princess with hair of ebon black, cheeks and lips of rosy

red, and a skin so fine and fair that she was called Snow White. But when the child was born the Queen died.

After a year had passed, the King married a second time. His new wife, who was now Queen, was very beautiful but haughty and proud and vain—indeed, her only wish in life was to be the fairest in the land. She had a mirror, a magic one, and when she looked in it she would say:

"Mirror, Mirror, on the wall,
Who's the fairest one of all?"

and the mirror would reply:

"Oh Queen, thou art the fairest in the land."

With this the Queen was well content for she knew that her mirror always spoke the truth.

The years flowed on, and all this time Snow White was growing up—and growing more beautiful each year besides. When she was seven years old she was fair as the day, and there came a time when the Queen stood in front of her mirror and said:

> "Mirror, Mirror, on the wall,
> Who's the fairest one of all?"

and this time the mirror answered:

> "Queen, thou art of beauty rare
> But Snow White with ebon hair
> Is a thousand times more fair."

At this the Queen became alarmed and turned green and yellow with envy. And whenever she saw Snow White after that, her heart turned upside down within her—that was how much she hated the innocent child for her beauty. These envious feelings grew like weeds in the heart of the Queen until she had no peace by day or by night. At last she could bear it no longer. She sent for a royal huntsman and told him to take the child into the woods and do away with her. "And bring me a token," she added, "so that I may be sure you've obeyed me."

SHE RAN ALL DAY THROUGH WOODS AND WOODS

So the huntsman called Snow White and led her into the woods but before he could harm her, she burst into tears and said, "Oh please, dear hunter, have mercy! If you will let me go, I'll gladly wander away, far away into the wildwood and I'll never come back again."

The huntsman was glad enough to help the sweet innocent girl, so he said, "Well, run away then, poor child, and may the beasts of the wood have mercy on you." As a token he brought back the heart of a wild boar, and the wicked Queen thought it was Snow White's. She had it cooked and ate it, I am sorry to say, with salt and great relish.

.   .   .   .   .

Little Snow White wandered off into the depths of the wildwood. Above her were leaves and leaves and leaves, about her the trunks of hundreds of trees, and she didn't know what to do. She began to run, over jagged stones and through thorny thickets. She passed many wild animals on the way, but they did not hurt her. She ran all day, through woods and woods and over seven high high hills. At last, just at sunset, she came upon a tiny hut in a wooded glen. The door was open and there was no one at home, so she thought she would stay and rest herself a little.

She went in and looked around. Everything was very small inside, but as neat and charming as could be, and very very clean. At one end of the room stood a table decked in

white, and on it were seven little plates, seven little knives and forks and spoons, and seven little goblets. In front of the table, each in its place, were seven little chairs; and at the far side of the room were seven beds, one beside the

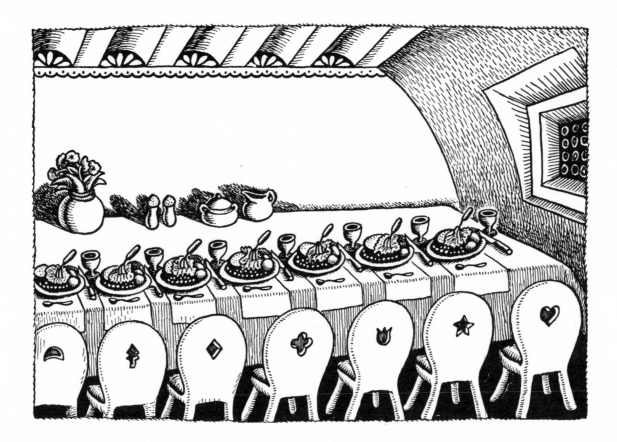

other, all made up with coverlets as pure and white as plum blossoms.

Snow White was hungry and thirsty, so she took from each little plate a bit of vegetable and a bite of bread, and from each little goblet a sip of sweet wine. She had become very tired, too, from all her running, and felt like taking a nap. She tried one bed after another but found it hard to choose the one which really suited her.

The first little bed was too hard.

The second little bed was too soft.

The third little bed was too short.

The fourth little bed was too narrow.

The fifth little bed was too flat.

The sixth little bed was too fluffy.

But the seventh little bed was just right so she lay down in it and was soon fast asleep.

After the sun had set behind the seventh hilltop and darkness had crept into the room, the masters of the little hut came home—they were seven little dwarfs who dug all day and hacked away at the hills, in search of gems and

gold. They lit their seven little lights and saw right away that someone had been there, for things were not quite the same as they had left them in the morning.

Said the first little dwarf, "Who's been sitting in my chair?"

Said the second little dwarf, "Who's been eating from my plate?"

Said the third, "Who's been nibbling at my bread?"

Said the fourth, "Who's been tasting my vegetables?"

Said the fifth, "Who's been eating with my fork?"

And the sixth, "Who's been cutting with my knife?"

And the seventh, "Who's been drinking from my little goblet?"

Now the first little dwarf turned around, and saw a hollow

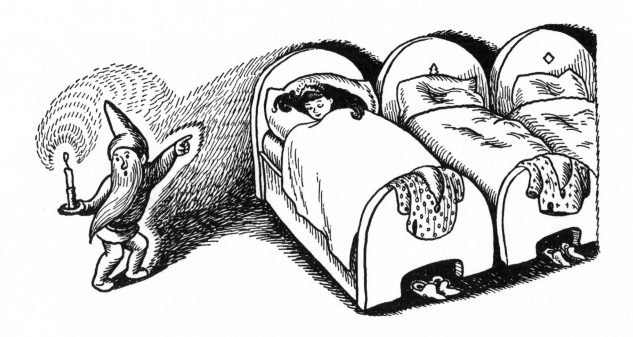

in his bed and said, "Someone's been sleeping in my bed."

And the second little dwarf looked at his bed and said, "Someone's been sleeping in mine too. It's rumpled."

And the third said, "In mine too, it's all humped up and crumpled."

And the fourth said, "In mine too. It's full of wrinkles."

And the fifth said, "And mine. It's full of crinkles."

And the sixth said, "Mine too. It's all tumbled up and jumbled."

But the seventh cried, "Well, someone's been sleeping in my bed, AND HERE SHE IS!"

The others came crowding around, murmuring and whispering in wonderment at the sight. "Ei! Ei!" they said, "how beautiful is this child!" They brought their tiny lights

and held them high, and looked and looked and looked. So pleased were they with their new little guest that they did not even wake her, but let her sleep in the bed all night. The seventh dwarf now had no bed, to be sure, but he slept with his comrades, one hour with each in turn until the night was over.

In the morning when Snow White awoke and saw seven little men tiptoeing about the room, she was frightened, but not for long. She soon saw that they were friendly little folk, so she sat up in bed and smiled at them. Now that she was awake and well rested. she looked more lovely than ever, with her rosy cheeks and big black eyes. The seven little

dwarfs circled round her in new admiration and awe, and said, "What is your name, dear child?"

"They call me Snow White," said she.

"And how did you find your way to our little home?" asked the dwarfs. So she told them her story.

All seven stood around and listened, nodding their heads and stroking their long long beards, and then they said, "Do you think you could be our little housekeeper—cook and knit and sew for us, make up our beds and wash our little clothes? If you will keep everything tidy and home-like, you can stay with us, and you shall want for nothing in the world."

"Oh yes, with all my heart!" cried Snow White. So there she stayed, and washed and sewed and knitted, and kept house for the kindly little men. Every day the seven dwarfs went off to one of the seven hills to dig for gems and gold. Each evening after sunset they returned, and then their supper had to be all ready and laid out on the table. But every morning before they left they would warn Snow White about the Queen.

"We don't trust her," they said. "One of these days she'll find out that you are here. So be careful, child, and don't let anyone into the house."

.   .   .   .   .   .

The dwarfs were right. One day the Queen, just to make sure, stood in front of her mirror and said:

"Mirror, Mirror, on the wall,
Who's the fairest **one of all?**"

and the mirror replied:

> "Thou art very fair, Oh Queen,
> But the fairest ever seen
> Dwells within the wooded glen
> With the seven little men."

The Queen turned green with fury when she heard this, for now she knew that the huntsman had deceived her, and that Snow White was still alive.

Day and night she sat and pondered, and wondered what to do, for as long as she was not the fairest in the land, her jealous heart gave her no rest. At last she thought out a plan: she dyed her face and dressed herself to look like a

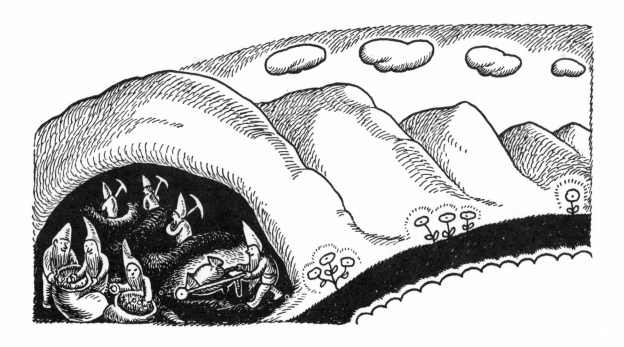

peddler woman. She did it so well that no one would have known her, and then, with a basketful of strings and laces, she made her way over the seven hills to the home of the seven dwarfs. When she reached it she knocked at the little door and cried, "Fine wares for sale! Fine wares for sale!"

Snow White peeped out of the window and said, "Good day, my dear woman, what have you there in your basket?"

"Good wares! Fine wares!" said the woman. "Strings, cords and laces, of all kinds and colors," and she held up a loop of gaily colored bodice laces.

Snow White was entranced with the gaudy trifle and she thought to herself, "The dwarfs were only afraid of the wicked Queen, but surely there can be no harm in letting

this honest woman into the house." So she opened the door and bought the showy laces.

"Child," said the woman as she entered the little room, "what a sight you are with that loose bodice! Come, let me fix you up with your new laces, so you'll look neat and trim for once."

Snow White, who suspected nothing, stood up to have the new gay laces put into her bodice, but the woman worked quickly and laced her up so tightly that Snow White lost her breath and sank to the floor.

"Now!" cried the Queen as she cast a last look at the motionless child, "now you have *been* the fairest in the land!"

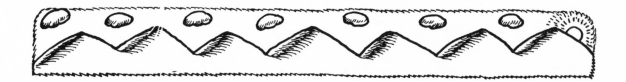

Luckily this happened just as the sun was sinking behind the seventh hill, so it was not long before the dwarfs came trudging home from work. When they saw their dear little Snow White lying there, not moving, not talking, they were deeply alarmed. They lifted her up, and when they saw how tightly she was laced, they hurriedly cut the cords in two. And in that moment Snow White caught her breath again, opened her eyes, and all was well once more.

When the dwarfs heard what had happened they said, "That was no peddler woman, Snow White; that was the wicked Queen. So please beware, dear child, and let no one into the house while we're gone."

. . . .

By this time the Queen had reached her home, so she rushed to her mirror and said:

"Mirror, Mirror, on the wall,
Who's the fairest one of all?"

and to her dismay it answered as before:

"Thou art very fair, Oh Queen,
But the fairest ever seen
Dwells within the wooded glen
With the seven little men."

At this the Queen's fury knew no bounds and she said,

"But now, my pretty one—now I'll think up something
which *will* be the end of you!" And soon she was very busy.

You will not be surprised, I am sure, when I tell you

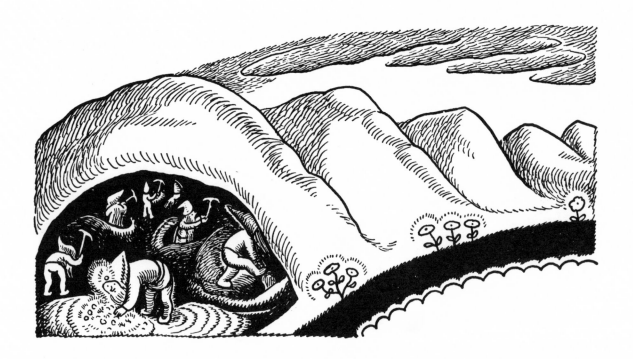

that this wicked creature was skilled in the arts of witch-craft; and with the help of these arts she now worked out her second scheme. She fashioned a comb—a beautiful golden comb, but a poisonous one. Then, disguising herself as a different old woman, she crossed the seven hills to the home of the seven dwarfs. When she reached it she knocked at the door and cried as before, "Good wares for sale! Fine wares! For sale! For sale!"

Snow White peeped out of the window but this time she said, "You may as well go on your way, good woman. I am not allowed to let anyone in."

"Very well!" said the old woman. "You needn't let me in, but surely there can be no harm in *looking* at my

wares," and she held up the glittering poisonous comb.

Snow White was so charmed by it that she forgot all about the dwarfs' warning and opened the door. The old woman stepped inside and said in honeyed tones, "Why don't you try it on right now, my little rabbit? Look, I'll show you how it should be worn!"

Poor Snow White, innocent and trusting, stood there with sparkling eyes as the woman thrust the comb into her ebon hair. But as soon as the comb touched her head, the poison began to work, and Snow White sank to the floor unconscious.

"You paragon of beauty!" muttered the Queen. "That will do for you, I think."

She hurried away just as the sun was sinking behind the seventh hill, and a few minutes later the dwarfs came trudging home from work. When they saw Snow White lying there on the floor, they knew at once that the Queen had been there again. Quickly they searched, and soon enough they found the glittering poisonous comb which was still

fastened in the girl's black hair. But at the very moment that they pulled it out, the poison lost its power and Snow White opened her eyes and sat up, as well as ever before.

When she told the seven dwarfs what had happened, they looked very solemn and said, "You can see, Snow White, it was not an old woman who came, but the wicked Queen in disguise. So please, dear child, beware! Buy nothing from anyone and let no one. no one at all, into the house while we're gone!"

And Snow White promised.

.   .   .   .   .

By this time the Queen had reached her home and there she stood in front of her mirror and said:

"Mirror, Mirror, on the wall,
Who's the fairest one of all?"

and the mirror answered as before:

"Thou art very fair, Oh Queen,
But the fairest ever seen
Dwells within the wooded glen
With the seven little men."

When she heard this, the Queen trembled with rage and disappointment. "I must, I *will* be the fairest in the land!" she cried, and away she went to a lonely secret chamber where no one ever came. There, by means of her wicked

witchery, she fashioned an apple. A very beautiful apple it was, so waxy white and rosy red that it made one's mouth water to look at it. But it was far from being as good as it looked, for it was so artfully made that half of it—the rosiest half—was full of poison.

When the Queen had finished this apple she put it into

a basket with some ordinary apples, and disguised herself as a peasant-wife. She crossed the seven hills to the home of the seven dwarfs and knocked at the door as before.

Snow White peeped out of the window and said, "I am not allowed to let anyone in, nor to buy anything either— the seven dwarfs have forbidden it."

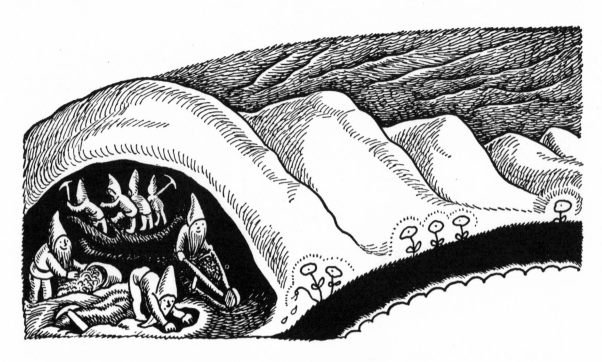

"Suits me," said the peasant-wife, "I can easily sell my
fine apples elsewhere. Here, I'll give you one for nothing."

"No," said Snow White, "I'm not allowed to take anything from strangers."

"Are you afraid? Of poison, perhaps?" said the woman.
"See, I'll cut the apple in two and I myself will eat half
of it to show you how harmless it is. Here, you can have
the nice rosy half, I'll take the white part."

By this time Snow White's mouth was fairly watering
for the luscious-looking fruit, and when the woman took a
big bite out of the white half and smacked her lips, the poor
girl could bear it no longer. She stretched her little hand
out through the window, took the rosy half of the apple and

bit into it. Immediately she sank to the floor and knew no more.

With a glance of glee and a laugh over-loud, the Queen cried, "Now, you! White as snow, red as blood and black as ebony—*now* let the dwarfs revive you!"

She could scarcely wait to get home to her mirror and say:

"Mirror, Mirror, on the wall,
 Who's the fairest one of all?"

and to her joy it said:

"Oh Queen, thou art the fairest in the land!"

Now there was peace at last in the heart of the Queen—

that is, as much peace as can ever be found in a heart full of envy and hate.

· · · · ·

After the wicked Queen had gone away, the sun sank down behind the seventh hill and the dwarfs came trudging home from work. When they reached their little home, no light gleamed from its windows, no smoke streamed from its chimney. Inside all was dark and silent—no lamps were lit and no supper was on the table. Snow White lay on the floor and no breath came from her lips.

At this sight the seven little dwarfs were filled with woe, for well they knew that this was once more the work of the wicked Queen.

"We must save her!" they cried, and hurried here and there. They lit their seven lights, then took Snow White and laid her on the bed. They searched for something poisonous but found nothing. They loosened her bodice, combed her hair and washed her face with water and wine, but nothing helped: the poor child did not move, did not speak, did not open her eyes.

"Alas!" cried the dwarfs. "We have done all we could, and now Snow White is lost to us forever!"

Gravely they shook their heads, sadly they stroked their beards, and then they all began to cry. They cried for three whole days and when at last they dried their tears, there lay Snow White, still motionless to be sure, but so fresh and rosy that she seemed to be blooming with health.

"She is as beautiful as ever," said the dwarfs to each other, "and although we cannot wake her, we must watch her well and keep her safe from harm."

So they made a beautiful crystal casket for Snow White

to lie in. It was transparent all over so that she could be seen from every side. On its lid they wrote in golden letters:

SNOW WHITE—A PRINCESS

and when it was all finished they laid Snow White inside and carried it to one of the seven hilltops. There they placed

it among the trees and flowers, and the birds of the wood came and mourned for her, first an owl, then a raven, and last of all a little dove.

Now only six little dwarfs went to dig in the hills every day, for each in his turn stayed behind to watch over Snow White so that she was never alone.

Weeks and months and years passed by, and all this time Snow White lay in her crystal casket and did not move or

open her eyes. She seemed to be in a deep deep sleep, her face as fair as a happy dream, her cheeks as rosy as ever. The flowers grew gaily about her, the clouds flew blithely above. Birds perched on the crystal casket and trilled and sang, the woodland beasts grew tame and came to gaze in wonder.

Some one else came too and gazed in wonder—not a bird or a rabbit or a deer, but a young Prince who had lost his way while wandering among the seven hills. When he saw the motionless maiden, so beautiful and rosy red, he looked and looked and looked. Then he went to the dwarfs and said, "Please let me take this crystal casket home with me and I will give you all the gold you may ask for."

But the dwarfs shook their heads and said, "We would not give it up for all the riches in the world."

At this the Prince looked troubled and his eyes filled with tears.

"If you won't take gold," he said, "then please give her to me out of the goodness of your golden hearts. I know not why, but my heart is drawn toward this beautiful Princess. If you will let me take her home with me, I will guard and honor her as my greatest treasure."

When they heard this, the kind little dwarfs took pity on the Prince and made him a present of Snow White in her beautiful casket.

The Prince thanked them joyfully and called for his servants. Gently they placed the crystal casket on their shoulders, slowly they walked away. But in spite of all their care, one of the servants made a false step and stumbled over a gnarly root. This joggled the casket, and the jolt

shook the piece of poisoned apple right out of Snow White's throat. And lo! she woke up at last and was as well as ever. Then all by herself she opened the lid, sat up, and looked about her in astonishment.

The Prince rushed up and lifted her out of the casket. He told her all that had happened and begged her to be his bride. Snow White consented with sparkling eyes, so they

rode away to the Prince's home where they prepared for a gay and gala wedding.

. . . . .

But while this was going on in the Prince's castle, something else was happening in that other castle where lived the wicked Queen. She had been invited to a mysterious wedding, so she dressed herself in her festive best and stood in front of her mirror and said:

"Mirror, Mirror, on the wall,
Who's the fairest one of all?"

and the mirror answered:

"Thou art very fair, Oh Queen,
But the fairest ever seen
Is Snow White, alive and well,
Standing 'neath a wedding bell."

When she heard this, the Queen realized that it was Snow White's wedding to which she had been invited. She turned purple with rage, but still she couldn't stay away. It would have been better for her if she had, for when she arrived she was given a pair of red hot shoes with which she had to dance out her wicked life. But as to all the rest—the Prince and his Princess Snow White, and the seven little dwarfs—they all lived happily ever after.

THE END

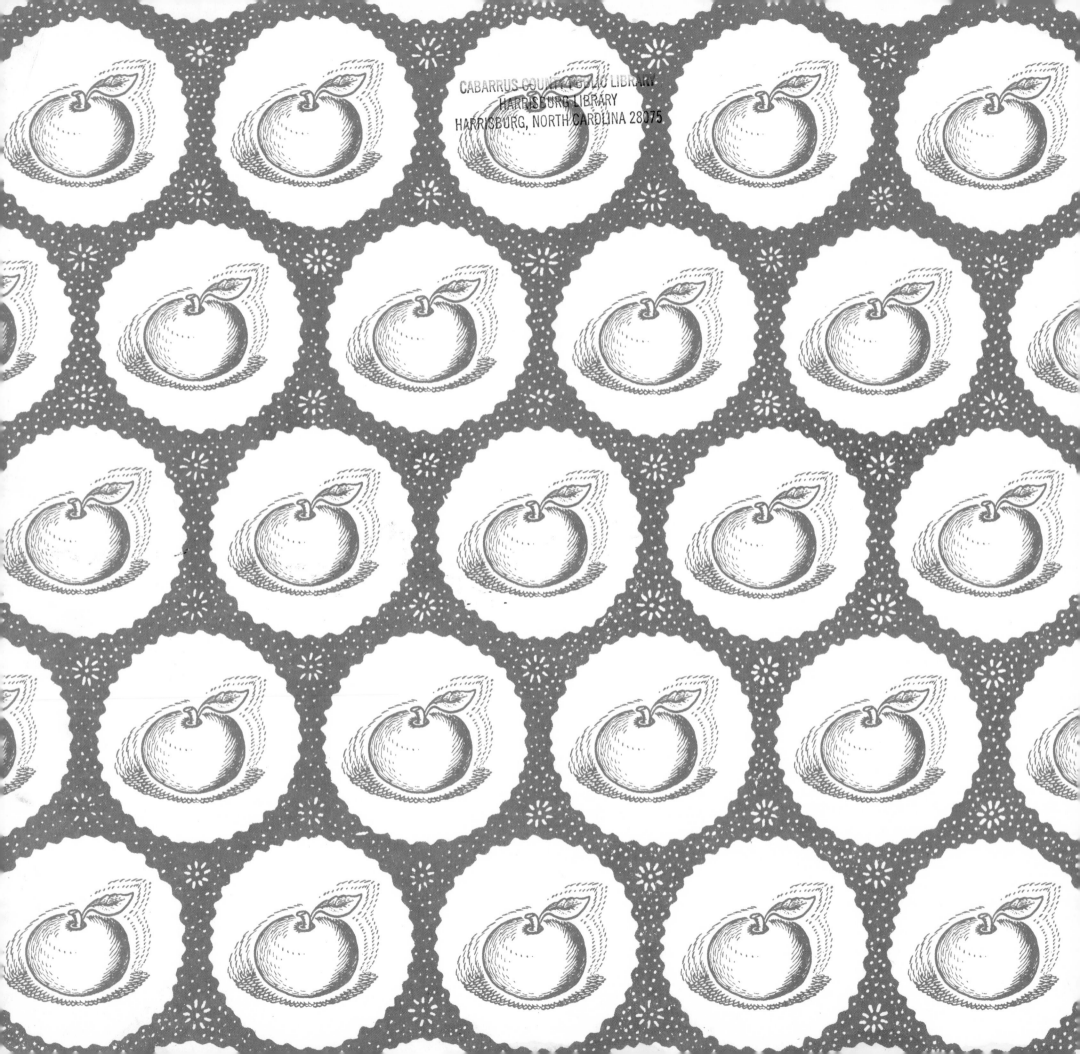